Reading Journal Response for Grades 6–8

by **Karen Soll**

Gail Saunders-Smith, PhD, consulting editor

capstone® classroom

1710 Roe Crest Drive,
North Mankato, Minnesota 56003
www.capstoneclassroom.com

Copyright © 2015 by Capstone Classroom, a division of Capstone.

All rights reserved. No part of this publication may be reproduced in whole or in part, or stored in a retrieval system, or transmitted in any form or by any means, electronic, mechanical, photocopying, recording, or otherwise, without written permission of the publisher. For information regarding permission, write to Capstone Classroom, 1710 Roe Crest Drive, North Mankato, Minnesota 56003.

Reading Journal Response for Grades 6–8

by Karen Soll

978-1-62521-958-9

Cover and Interior Design: Jodi Pedersen

Cover image from Shutterstock

Table of Contents

INTRODUCTION 4
JOURNAL RESPONSES. 5
   I would/wouldn't recommend this book because 5
   An inference I made while reading this book was 6
   The theme or central idea of this book is. 7
   This book is about 8
   I agree/disagree with the author's point of view, which is 9
   The author used figurative language, such as. 10
   This book reminded me of. 11
   This book is similar to another that I read. 12
   One of the characters helped move the story along by. 13
   If I were one of the characters or people in the book 14
   This book presented information in a way 15
   This is a history/science book that described a process. 16
   New words and definitions I learned include 17
   The charts and diagrams the author used 18
   This book reminded me of a science experiment 19
   Two characters or events can be compared. They are. 20
   A confusing part of the book was 21
   This genre of this book is. 22
   I would rewrite the ending by. 23
JOURNAL RESPONSE LOG 24

Introduction

A child's connection to reading can be strengthened with a short writing activity after the book has been read. This book includes several journal responses from which to choose. Responses are included for nonfiction and fiction books and some may even be adapted for poetry and plays. Select the journal response that is most appropriate, and give your child time to write a short response to the prompt.

If your child is struggling to come up with a response, do some pre-writing. As your child prepares to write, talk about some ideas he or she might include. Have your child make a list of these ideas and talk about how he or she can craft the ideas into sentences. You can also ask questions that get a little deeper, such as, "What excited you?" or "What were you thinking as we read this part?"

If your child is a reluctant writer, here are some quick tips you could try:

- Ask your child questions that may help him or her write the answer.
- Ask your child to connect the book to his or her life, and ask how.
- Allow your child to use the computer to respond.

Help make the writing activity fun by allowing your child to respond to whatever he or she related to. When reviewing your child's work, respond to the content of his or her writing rather than the mechanical errors. Journal writing should be viewed as a quick, fun way to give an opinion or extend the learning.

A log has been included at the end of this guide. We recommend that you fill it in whenever your child responds to a text.

Journal Response

Title of Book _____ Date _____

I would/wouldn't recommend this book because ...

Journal Response

Title of Book _____ Date _____

An inference I made while reading this book was ...

Journal Response

Title of Book _____ Date _____

The theme or central idea of this book is ...

The part of the book that helped me realize this is ...

Journal Response

Title of Book _____ Date _____

This book is about ...

Journal Response

Title of Book _____ Date _____

I agree/disagree with the author's point of view, which is ...

Journal Response

Title of Book _____ Date _____

The author used figurative language, such as ...

It was an effective/ineffective way to describe ...

Journal Response

Title of Book _____ Date _____

This book reminded me of ...

Journal Response

Title of Book _____ Date _____

This book is similar to another that I read, except this one provided more/less information about ...

Journal Response

Title of Book _____ Date _____

One of the characters helped move the story along by ...

Journal Response

Title of Book _____ Date _____

If I were one of the characters or people in the book, I would have ...

because ...

Journal Response

Title of Book _____ Date _____

This book presented information in a way that made/didn't make sense because it ...

Journal Response

Title of Book _____ Date _____

This is a history/science book that described a process.
The key steps of the process include ...

Journal Response

Title of Book _____ Date _____

New words and definitions I learned include ...

Journal Response

Title of Book _____ Date _____

The charts and diagrams the author used helped/didn't help because ...

Journal Response

Title of Book _____ Date _____

This book reminded me of a science experiment I did because ...

Journal Response

Title of Book _____ Date _____

Two characters or events can be compared. They are ...

Journal Response

Title of Book _____ Date _____

A confusing part of the book was ...

Journal Response

Title of Book _____ Date _____

This genre of this book is _____

I know because ...

Journal Response

Title of Book _____ Date _____

I would rewrite the ending by ...

Journal Response Log

Date	Title of Book	Response